THE GLASGOW KISS

THE GLASGOW KISS

The wrong and right way to use your head

Caroline Neeley

iUniverse, Inc.

New York Lincoln Shanghai

The Glasgow KISS
The wrong and right way to use your head

iUniverse books may be ordered through booksellers or by contacting:

iUniverse
2021 Pine Lake Road, Suite 100
Lincoln, NE 68512
www.iuniverse.com
1-800-Authors (1-800-288-4677)

ISBN-13: 978-0-595-38577-5 (pbk)
ISBN-13: 978-0-595-82956-9 (ebk)
ISBN-10: 0-595-38577-X (pbk)
ISBN-10: 0-595-82956-2 (ebk)

Printed in the United States of America

To Sarah and Scott,
You bring me love and happiness every day of my life.

Contents

What They Are Saying

You are honest and affectionately direct in helping me be honest with myself. Our crossing of paths has enabled me to redirect myself in ways I never thought possible. Your non-judgmental style gave me a safe place to face my shortcomings and learn to deal with my issues in a healthy way. The results are tangible.

—Michele, a client—

What an inspirational person you are! Thanks for taking care of us. You're always so positive and upbeat. My daughter wants to be just like you.

—a Radio Station KVTA AM 1520, Ventura, CA., listener—

Thank you for being such a valuable "champion" for our school. The kids love it when you come and speak to them about being nice to each other and influence them with your positive outlook on being a child. Oh, and they love your accent!

—*Pleasant Valley School District, Camarillo, CA., educator*—

I feel differently once I speak with you. I can't thank you enough for not only your services but as a person who really cares.

—*Marsha, a divorced mother of one*—

I appreciate all you have done for my granddaughter. She really enjoys you.

—*Marion, proud grandmother*—

Thank you for your great ideas and helping my family through the hardships and difficulties that divorce blankets over us. My former wife and I are working together to make the transition a little bit easier of our children. Your direct no nonsense approach helped us through each and every step.

—*David, a client*—

Author's Note

To those of us who have ever set out on a lifelong journey to "find yourself," there is one most humbling way to do it. Write a book. I named this book *The Glasgow KISS* for one very simple reason. It fits.

In my native homeland of Scotland, a "Glasgow Kiss" is a brief, albeit heated argument, with one or two shoulder butts, followed by one disputant unsuspectingly head-butting the other, knocking him to the ground, dazed. Hence, this is known as giving him a "kiss."

Since I grew up in Glasgow, the kiss is dubbed the *Glasgow Kiss*. Other cities called it their kiss. Somewhat dazed on the ground, each would help the other to their feet, dust each other off and inquire, "*Yuh awe right, Jimmy?*" The name Jimmy, is a Scottish endearing nickname for guys. Girls are called "hens". Shake hands and offer to buy a pint of beer or a shot of their favorite beverage. By all accounts the conflict is over. Quickly started, quicker finished. All better. Or is it?

I do not profess to be the author John Grisham or even Dr. Phil McGraw—maybe more of a wee touch of Dr. Seuss, to be more accurate. But I am enthusiastic and passionate about getting my thoughts, insight and advice onto the written page.

In my private practice as an Anger Management and Mediation counselor in Ventura County, California, I have seen it all. With my local radio show I have heard it all. You can access my website, www.neeleymediation.com, click on events and appearances for current information. From the high school sophomore who has shut down in the face of her fears towards her disapproving parents to the husband who, with deer in the headlights resolve, darkens my doorway to talk about his failed marriage.

To be sure, these are not stories for exploitation. There are no names and, as it is with all of us in this genre of practice, anonymity is the cornerstone of our work.

But with each turn of the page, I trust you will see yourself, someone you love, someone you once knew or someone you may meet along the stumbling blocks in the road of life.

I have taken great pains—literally and figuratively—to write this book for the lay reader who might never have the guts, the courage, the inclination or the openness to make an appointment to drop by my office. Lucky for you, I am bringing the closed door session to you. No charge. No referral discounts. Just come on in. Read as much or as little as you want. Tell me as much or as little as you want.

This book is not a replacement for therapy. If you feel you need more in-depth assistance, counseling or more hands-on one-on-one help, go to your phone book and find a health professional in your area. Or, you can always email me at www.neeleymediation.com for more information as to how to locate the appropriate counselor.

Each chapter is designed for brevity and browsing. Linger awhile when I hit on a nerve. Skim through when you need to move on. The chapters are not building blocks from page one to the end. They are for your savoring. For your thought-provoking action, in any order you see fit. So sit back on my couch and tell me all about it. It's quiet here. The counselor is in.

Acknowledgements

No one ever achieves much without the help and support of others and creating this book was no exception. From the time I decided to write *The Glasgow KISS*, through its many drafts, re-writes, and finally the editing, publishing and promotion, I have been privileged with the encouragement and support of so many precious and wonderful people. I would like to publicly acknowledge a few to whom I am particularly grateful.

My precious teenagers, Sarah and Scott who stand with me every day, are a pillar of strength on either side. Your continuous love and support in the creation and finally the conclusion of this book made me the "Energizer© Bunny."

Thank you, Dad and Mum, Tommy and Betty Davis for all the support and encouragement—and on occasion, a good kick up the bum when I needed it. No one in the whole could have better parents than me. I am what I am today because of you. Thanks, Mum, for not allowing me to throw in the towel no matter how much I complained. And Dad, your endearing Scottish phrase *"Baer Up Bairn"* keeps me going when times get rough.

Tommy Davis, Jr., and Elizabeth Connolly, my big brother and wee sister, without the open, generous and profoundly honest conversations we had during this endeavor and still do, I doubt I could have written so well. Tommy, you never doubted my ability to accomplish great things. I am almost as *"great"* as you. Elizabeth, you are always there when I need you, day or night, weekends, too.

I am fortunate to have friends of substance and loyalty, without whom life would be more difficult. I especially want to acknowledge Troy and Danny Rather, my sushi buddies, for keeping me sane, sometimes in spite of myself. The next trip to the sushi bar is on me.

My editor Sherill Whisenand whose honesty and straight forwardness kept me on my toes, I thank you. I respect you immensely so much that I am doubly tickled when a sentence doesn't get the red pen treatment.

If a picture is worth a thousand words, my photographer Mike Burley is worth a million *oohs* and *ahhs*. His ability to capture the perfect moment in a less-than-perfect world is a testament to his professionalism and vast repertoire.

My book cover graphic artist Wes Bredall, thank you for being so patient with me and the endless changes I had you do because I am so picky. You never complained and wanted perfection as much as I did. You are the greatest.

And finally my listening audience—on the radio and in book form. Thank you for allowing me into your lives. I am grateful for the opportunity to do something of value. I work daily to live up to your expectations.

—Caroline Neeley

Introduction

You become quite discouraged with yourself after you have had an argument with a family member, a neighbor or a boss. That's life. But after everything is said and done there is always something you wished you had said further to bolster your argument. It could pertain to you or in defense of someone else.

Why does this happen? Why is it that we wished we had said more? By your very nature, you do not like conflict or if you find yourself in it, you cannot handle it well. To make your point with clarity causes you stress, a feeling of ineptness. Another common reason you do not defend yourself is because of the fear of the unknown. The outcome is too scary, coupled with trepidation of confrontation and consequences. Those consequences are that you are being viewed as a loser. Your friends might not talk to you anymore. You will simply not get what you want.

You want to be liked so you turn deaf, dumb and blind to the reality that there are people out there who really just do not like you. They never have. They never will. And who cares? You do! It surely is a hard pill to swallow and even more difficult to learn to accept it so we tend to keep our mouths shut in the hope that the fewer waves we make, the more people will like us. Hardly true.

The Glasgow KISS is an outpouring of my ability to bring you some ideas and tools to reconstruct your deflated confidence and offer constructive suggestions. The obvious outcome is to give you direction to fight fair for what is right for your circumstances without compromising all your beliefs.

I will help you create your working boundaries and will teach you how to keep your boundary lines clear of toxic waste, known as other's perceptions of the world and of you. Some will read this book for the self-help aspect. Others seek guidance in dealing with difficult family members including teenagers who grew from chubby cheeks to mouthy maniacs in record time. Some of you are givers and want to offer solace and direction to others.

There might be a time you lack the courage to follow through with your threats, your actions, your unfair treatment and those not-so-silent dreams. When you lack the courage to follow through in what you say and do, you simply allow others to take advantage of your inconsistencies, turn them around, twist them up, unfold them and use those inconsistencies against you.

We are creatures of comfortable compatibility. We gravitate to those we can count on, dependable to a fault. But when you are confronted with a person who has created a pattern of not following through, why take them seriously?

You will learn how to build your pillar of courage to follow through and accept that not all people are going to agree with you. Isn't that a hard lesson to learn? Not everyone sees things your way. If you have given circumstance enough thought before taking action on it, you are making the right decision for you, who then, has the right to question it? No one. And no other opinion counts. You answer only to yourself. Consider yourself an asset in anyone's life. If they are blind to you as an asset but view you as a detriment, then they are not worthy of your qualities, time and desires. Consider it their loss. *"Next!"*

I am not a fan of psycho-babble. There are too many therapists, psychologists and other mental health professionals ready to take your hard earned cash and spout words that you have never heard before. Most words probably do not exist in our daily lexicon. The counselors sound very intelligent with their five hundred-dollar words. I seriously doubt the mental health professionals understand what they just said to you. I believe the only way to reconstructing your esteem is to look in the mirror, identify what you see and review the changes to be made. The first big secret: make those changes with embraced enthusiasm!

You will not read here or see me dredging up twenty years of your past history to discover why you did what you did or said what you said. The past is the past. The past does not equal your future. History cannot be changed no matter how long ago. The past cannot change the present. You can learn from past experiences but the past doesn't change. It is called history for a reason. As the old saying goes, *"Yesterday is history, tomorrow is a mystery and today is a gift."*

There will be no psycho-babble from me and you are not even paying for the house call! ***The Glasgow KISS*** is pointed and direct. You will not need to read half the book to suddenly get a question answered. When a question pops into your head you will be able to go to that chapter and find your answer. It will be easy reading and magically simple to understand.

It is my hope that you are elevated to a higher level of self-reliance and independence. Walk evermore around with the air of royalty, the strength of a conqueror and the will of a warrior soldier.

Enjoy.

Now Where Did I Last See Myself?

('Finding Myself' is a ridiculous myth)

I wonder if you are thinking this chapter, based on its title, is going to be some psycho-analysis of "finding yourself?" If so, sorry folks, you would be out of luck. Read on and you will discover where my views and thoughts are on "finding yourself." I warn you, though, I am not a fan of intentional confusion!

When someone tells you they need to go *find themselves,* what are they really saying? Have they somehow disconnected from their body and they need to go find it? Are they searching in the lost and found box?

"Finding myself" is pure psycho-babble. I simply will not tolerate that kind of talk and rationalization. Psycho-babble is memorizing million dollar words and throwing them out like a wild night on the town. A great number of clinical professionals mean to confuse us more because they do not know the answer themselves.

By the time many of my clients and others arrive at my doorstep seeking relief, their heads are spinning so fast in the bowls of confusion because of these professional psycho-babblers. Therefore making my tangible and realistic approach seem like a language conjured up by extra-terrestrials. In the brief time clients spend with me they leave learning more about themselves than all those years of babble. What is wrong with that picture? *Psycho-babble* is just wrong.

Indirectly though, "finding myself" has become a verbalization for simply wanting to be found, but in a psychological way. Let's analyze this phrase, "finding myself." No doubt you will see yourself in one of two scenarios:

Scenario 1:
Quite often you are faced with a conundrum and you do not have an answer readily at hand. You must disconnect from someone or something to give yourself some time to clarify the decision or find an equitable solution, giving more thought to the conclusion or outcome.

Scenario 2:
You do not want to deal with an uncomfortable situation. You are quite content, shifting the responsibility and consequences to someone else. By using the term "finding yourself," you have chosen to opt out of acknowledging any responsibility and created a temporary deterrent and avoidance of the inevitable.

Both scenarios on the surface appear difficult to accomplish, right? But if you look closer, scenario 1 is requiring a moment to think deeper about your decision. Deep down and instinctively you have made the right decision but because this could be a new adventure, you are naturally a little uncertain and need some confirmation and clarity. Automaker Henry Ford once said: "*Failure is the opportunity to begin again more intelligently.*" You are willing to take the chance.

Scenario 2 is a complete denial of an existing "problem," something you are regularly guilty of—or as guys like to use, "issue."

When someone chooses to avoid the obvious or shifts the obvious to someone else they are building an impression of weakness and insecurity. They cannot handle a crisis well. They are definitely not a leader but someone who can only handle the less complicated challenges that life might throw your way. Are you someone who can hold on to lasting relationships? Probably not. People, by their very nature, appreciate strength and value as a solid foundation of one's self.

With which scenario do you best identify? Are you a confident individual, facing a temporary moment of confusion? Or are you a weakling, perpetually avoiding awkward and embarrassing situations because you do not want to look bad or confront? Are you afraid to challenge the outcome? Predictably, you will leave the circumstance open ended for someone else to face the consequences whether it's favorable or not.

Obviously, you would choose the first scenario. Ideally, that is how you want to be viewed and known by others. I do not believe for one minute that there are people out there who are okay with being viewed as a weak, zero confidence, immature individual, whose life is in absolute chaos because they can not affirm that in fact the sky is blue, right?

You have the potential for being strong, independent and self-assured. When you avoid confrontations by refusing to stand up for what you believe is right, over time people will abuse, take advantage and even exploit your insecurity. Sadly, some people choose to go through life in a state of avoidance. Why? It is easier to bear, and carries little effort. The downside is though, people like this they have little to be proud, lacking hard-earned self-accomplishments and often feel cheated out of what life has to offer. Life is full of daily challenges.

Which scenario do you want to be? How can you become Scenario 1? Dump the psycho-babble, "finding yourself," please! You know how you are. You know your likes and dislikes. You also know how far someone can push you before you reach your breaking point. Is this correct? Okay then. That is the first step. You have to acknowledge that you know yourself a little better than you want to believe. You do have boundaries you will allow people to cross—or more often than not, not cross.

Scenario 2 sadly, is the majority of the population. People are choosing more and more to not get involved in anyone's business. It is much easier to turn a blind eye to the mother in the grocery store chastising her child loudly and depositing a swift slap on his legs because she's having a bad day, or the young couple arguing at full volume in the restaurant causing uneasiness for the other diners, out to enjoy a relaxing drink, tasty meal and good company.

Either way, people avoid situations that can cause self embarrassment, fear of being ridiculed or chastised. Why? It is because of the unrest. Regardless of where it happens and who it involves does not directly impact you, you are choosing *not* to make it your business.

So, now ask yourself again, "Would I rather be viewed as the person who stood up and defended the child being slapped? Or asked the arguing couple to take it outside so as to not draw any more attention to their behavior? Or be the person who sat back mumbling, 'What a disgrace! How embarrassing!' finding solace in "It's not my business?"

Remember, you have to live with yourself—and all your accomplishments and failures. On the other hand, you can "find yourself," the real you, by not listening to psycho babblers' empty words of hope. Get out there and act! Words are hollow and meaningless unless they are followed by actions.

PLAYING THE BLAME GAME

Much like people, blame comes in all shapes and sizes. But it is unanimous that shifting blame for your own inadequacies or mistakes onto others releases you from responsibility and consequences. When you allow others to shift blame and permit them to be unburdened by it, you are no better than they are. Fault and failure are still not being dealt with.

Ultimately you make your own choices—whether it is bearing the burdens of others faults or cowardly shifting blame so you will not look bad. Either way, ask yourself, "How valuable and credible am I if I allow this behavior to continue?"

Is it true that when we hear stories of blame either way, we are horrified and disgusted that someone could be so self-doubting and unsure of them self that the sheer lack of confidence is preventing them from going into defense mode? Is someone so narcissistic that the mere thought of accepting one ounce of blame would send them to the psychiatric hospital? They do what we call *shifting*.

A young woman who stayed in a five-year relationship with a volatile abusive boyfriend who was not nice to her for no apparent reason. She stated that he would call her "fat," even though she is a light-weight at 108 pounds. She was called stupid, anti-social, had no fashion sense and the list goes on.

Why would she stay? It is that tied and true female mentality. As with many, she believed she could *fix* him. She continued to take the abuse because she thought things would get better over time. But *fixing him* meant she had to be even more submissive and continue to do what she was told, rather than seeking a nice guy. I have to ask you: what is wrong with dating a nice guy rather than spending time and energy trying to fix a broken one? The answer is comfort and familiarity—even if that comfort is unhealthy.

It is so typical of women to stay in unhealthy relationships, all the while blindly attacking the man because their personal needs are not being met. They never learn enough about themselves to want to change their own life first. But women consistently and intentionally put themselves in situations that no amount of effort and time will change anything. The alternative is accepting the unhealthiness and ignoring the fear of the unknown.

If you are okay with this, by all means remain unhealthy but do not expect emotional wealth and happiness to kick in somewhere down the road. It will not change unless you make the first move and have the courage to follow through on the right order of value. You have to muster up the courage and move into unfamiliar territory without fear and welcome the challenge.

What the young lady should be doing is spending time trying to find out what it is about herself that makes her want to stay in a dysfunctional relationship. Accept and acknowledge that when fixing is not asked for and not wanted, taking on the responsibility of "*it must be my fault*" is misplaced blame.

Where is the logic in any man or woman who chooses to stay with someone who is consistently mean? Don't tell me it is because "*you care.*" If that were true and caring was used in the true meaning of the word then you are cheating yourself out of happiness and contentment. To be consistently mean and hostile, frankly, there would be no justifiable reason other than self-control and domination, right? A real man would not treat his girlfriend this way.

I received a call at the radio station from a 19-year-old girl who was complaining that her parents would not invite her current boyfriend over for dinner. Her exact words were, "*They are being so unfair and selfish. He's such a nice guy!*" As it turns out, this "nice guy" was 28 years old, dating a 19-year-old girl! But let's not rush to judgment. Give him another chance? He is twice divorced and has a 3-year-old son.

I quickly cut in, "*Why would a seemingly nice guy be divorced twice at the ripe old age of 28 and has a son he hardly sees? His first wife cheated on him and his second wife said he was a workaholic,*" she claimed. Of course, this is a one sided conversation intended to lure an immature, impressionable young girl into the sordid web of a guy who most likely cannot handle a woman but can mold a girl to his liking.

As I explained to her, "*His world revolves around his wants, needs and desires only. When his requirements and expectations are not met he moves on and hunts down someone like you who is vulnerable and who wants so badly to be all grown up. And when his needs are no longer being met he will dump you too. He's a wolf on the prowl for a lamb. Guess who his latest innocent, pure little lamb is? Oh, and by the way, your parents see the predator in him and are only trying to protect you from hurt.*"

I remember one of the very first cases I handled. I was mediating a couple's divorce and settling an equitable split in assets and community property. The wife and husband were entwined in a bitter divorce and custody battle initiated by the wife. The couple had been married for eight years but for the last two the unification had become toxic and was rapidly deteriorating mainly because of the husband's verbally abuse, lack of accepting any kind of responsibility for the abuse and on two occasions had been physically violent with his wife.

He was used to getting his way, a trend that reluctantly his wife had to admit she was a frequent contributor. He was always going to be the king of his castle and everyone else was categorized as a pawn. In his castle he could do no wrong. It was everyone else, *never* him. In all eight years of marriage she could not recall even once her husband apologizing for any hurt feeling, condescension or remotely exhibiting once ounce of remorse. The wife believed that respect could not be found anywhere in her husband's memory banks even if she searched the deepest darkest corner of his vault. It simply did not exist.

I was daring and confident enough to challenge this mighty king by attempting to tear down his castle called divorce. He let me know more than once via his body language, facial expressions and words that a battle was brewing and I would be the one to retreat in shreds—definitely behaviors of intimidation to a tadpole desperately trying to rush the circle of life and become a frog as quickly as possible.

As the process moved forward emotions heightened and our sessions were becoming more volatile. As much as I tried to defuse repeated explosive bouts of anger and frustration from him, I was at a loss as to how to proceed without coming away from these negotiations completely deflated and defeated.

I shared with my parents that I was working on a particularly difficult case, primarily because it was one of my first, and that I was perplexed as to how to proceed in a constructive manner. Without violating confidentiality, I told my parents that one of the parties was intensely volatile, loud and obnoxious.

My parents in their usual way, told me to "take it like a man." Now this kind of statement coming from my dad to his daughter could be interpreted as sexist, but of course none intended. What he meant was I should not buckle under pressure and never allow anyone to control a situation especially when it is occurring on my battle field. But of course, being very Scottish, what I heard from him was *"Don't physically give him/her The Glasgow Kiss. Dish it out mentally, aim straight and hit them between the eyes."* And I did.

With my *Glasgow Kiss* attitude I entered into the next round of negotiations with an iron fist, a well-planned strategy and confidence that could have stopped the English from invading Scotland in 1014. William Wallace would have been proud.

The next series of meetings with them were conducted with a firm hand and little room for aggression. Prior to each meeting, independent of the wife, I made it very clear to him that I was the one running this show and I would not tolerate hostility—regardless of who initiated the aggression or antagonism. At the very onset I would shut the meeting down and would hold him financially responsible for my allotted time.

The fact of the matter is you are always going to encounter selfish, self-absorbing, socio-path, narcissistic people who will burden you with their guilt and lack of morality and sense. You cannot control them but you can control yourself and your environment and circumstances you choose to put yourself in. How well you maintain a level of composure and control in times of conflict and clash ultimately makes you the stronger person.

The bottom line is do not be one of these people I mentioned here. Elevate yourself to higher standards of value and stop playing their blame game. Accept responsibility and blame where it is due and defend yourself whenever necessary and appropriate.

Pick your battles and choose non-confrontational words. Take a brief moment to think about what you want to say *before* you open your mouth because once the hostile words are out, it is really difficult to take them back. Your point will still be made but you will save yourself the aggravation.

Listen to what others have to say. It does not mean you have to agree. It is okay to disagree on a certain subject matters. Case in point, my daughter Sarah is accepting of same sex marriages. I am not. Nevertheless, to Sarah, her points are valid and *bona fide*. Both of us understand and are clear that on this subject, we greatly differ but know that the diversity in this area could never destroy our relationship.

It is amazing how much more you discover about someone and how deeper a conversation can become when you are willing to listen to every word and not select only the favorable ones.

BEND OVER BACKWARDS AND SET YOUR BOUNDARIES

Most of us by nature, bend over backwards for those we care about. We will pour out empathy to those who need a moment of compassion, a tender touch or a shoulder to cry on.

Most of us harbor good sense, caring foundation and kindness directed at those who we love, and the unknown man or woman walking in the street. To be kind is genuinely in our blood. It comes naturally. But when caring and kindness becomes a chore, (do I dare to say fake it?) where do you draw the line? Where do you draw your personal boundaries?

It is so important to set personal boundaries, not solely for the purpose of others, but for you. When you set boundaries for yourself and stick to them with the knowledge that once or twice you will stray or wander from your guidelines, just don't stray too far.

However, if you are the type of person who can stay on track without much difficulty your boundaries are circled safely around you and you have nothing to worry about. No one ever wants to permanently lose that old innate gene used for nurturing, caring and wanting to fix everything. Remember, you can only fix what wants fixing.

Boundaries allow you to manage your self-control. Those around you with whom you regularly interact will always have clarity as to where you stand on issues. You will begin to feel less vulnerable in communication and more content with yourself, secure and confident in your decisions.

You are refusing to sweat the small stuff anymore. Trust me on this. You will be happier and people will develop greater respect for you. You will be seen as a definite clear decision maker. Choose to live your life in black and white. Commit to memory that gray is only for the weak and those who do not want to deal with the challenges and consequences of black and white.

You have to agree that having the capability to control your emotions at the flip of a switch is quite powerful and intriguing. It is so physically draining being stuck on the emotional rollercoaster. Have comfort knowing where you are going and with whom you are sharing the journey or when you plan on returning.

What are boundaries? Boundaries are rules, regulations, policies, guidelines, whatever you want to call them. You develop them for yourself to maintain some level of cautiousness and control. Building boundaries is not an easy task. How tightly wound do you want these boundaries to be? Tight enough there is little room to move around. You are firm in your decision. There is no negotiation room. People soon learn that they need not bother challenging you on anything if there is absolutely no wiggle room.

Or do you loosely wrap your self-created boundaries giving the outward impression that you know what you want and will not allow anyone to stand in your way? Or are you really saying when push comes to shove you will probably give in like you've done so many times before? Admit to yourself that maybe you could be afraid of the outcome. It is just too scary to bare the responsibility.

When you contribute to bettering yourself, as selfish as that sounds, it is okay, because you are the one who needs to find out what really makes you tick. Before you begin to create boundaries, you must first acknowledge your position within your family, close friends, business, etc.

Are you a wife or husband, a mother or father, sister or brother, co-worker, someone's boss? Ask yourself, "How much do these people mean to me?" How much do I mean to them?" Are they important enough that I am willing to show them the true me by giving them the opportunity to understand me?" and "Do I show them my life?"

Resolve to keep that circle of closeness to certain people who are worth the effort and are good for you. Examine your likes, dislikes, and tolerance levels. Most importantly, how many times do you give into someone or succumb to temptation and regret it later? Misplaced temptation is the most difficult to overcome. Why? It is difficult to break a habit. When you are so used to acting or thinking a certain way it is difficult to break that habit or even change it a little.

Have you ever heard of someone kicking their addiction or habit in 48 or 72 hours? It never happens. When people go into rehabilitation to break an addiction, the average stay is 21 days. It takes most people 21 days to overcome the craving of an addiction or act in a certain way which has been deemed a detriment. The remaining time in rehab is, by and large, used to ensure the dependency for the most part is gone and the building of confidence and self-control can begin.

You have learned to stay clear of your addiction or habit. So why would setting personal boundaries be any easier if you have never had them to begin with?

We all have a powerful and influential mind. Why waste it on past regretful things? How sad it is to refuse to open your mind to the beautiful things that life has to offer and allow people to see you as a valuable asset. People only see what you allow them to see. If you consistently show people your negative side, why would anyone want to be around or come home to you? If you take time and make the effort to seek out goodness in people, by highlighting their values and qualities, you will soon find yourself being hunted down for company. Offer ripe fruit not rotting fruit. Bees are attracted to honey—not manure and for good reason.

Imagine that the boundary you have set for yourself as a circle of warm, blue crystal clear water, completely engulfing you. Someone comes along and is attempting to splash in your water by saying or doing something that usually would be upsetting. Rather than waiting for that small irritant to manifest itself into an explosive bomb, nip it in the bud at the onset of the splashing in *your* warm, blue crystal clear water.

If you continue to defend your boundaries in a positive constructive way, people know exactly where they stand with you. No more guess work or walking on egg shells. You will feel like a warrior soldier, ready to take on the world.

No crystal ball, magic wand or sprinkling of fairy dust will be administered here. Use your beautiful mind to make it happen and understand that you are capable all along of this accomplishment.

Drain the Emotional Bathtub... I'm Drowning!

Everyone feels stress at times. It can be caused by other's perceptions and their circumstances. Some feel it more than others. But it is how well *you* deal with stress that can also dictate how well you manage your life and your emotions.

Any physician will tell you that stress is the emotional and physiological reaction to a threat, whether real or imagined, resulting in a series of adaptations by our bodies. I am a big fan of simplicity. Life is not supposed to be complicated but it does have its twists and turns. I would prefer medical professionals would lay off making a diagnosis sound so complex. I want the same information but in a simpler form.

What you really want the physician to tell you when you are feeling stressed out is: "*I am completely overwhelmed and I am allowing myself to go nuts.*" And, "*Slow down and try to relax. I am going to give myself a heart attack! Gather my thoughts.*" The reality of stress is that you have piled too much food on your plate and now the food is beginning to fall off. You are simply having a momentary lapse in organization. See how simple that is? Be direct. Don't confuse me, you say.

Everyone knows when they have reached their maximum stress load. You do not need the doctor to tell you that. The stress today may have been caused by your current job. Maybe you have an overwhelming number of projects and not enough time to complete them. Your boss is a jackass and your children are driving you crazy. Big deal! Your patience is in short supply and you are irritable. Your heart rate is up and you are slowly burning out. Your usual high performance and productivity is slowly slipping away. Yes, you are drowning.

The trick in allowing yourself to rehash over and over despairing levels of stress is to learn to *manage* it. Or you could continue to stress out and eventually suffer a heart attack, psychological distress, consistent fatigue, uncontrollable hostility and anxiety, just to mention a few. Who wants to come home each night to that? I know I would not.

I want to share methods and ways to relax yourself, pull yourself together and gather your thoughts. It is very important to take some time for *you*!

Find your temper, before you lose it. There is just no need to be counterproductive by yelling, throwing things and swearing. These emotional outbursts have an immediate effect on those in your line of fire. It will cause them to shut down and be silent. They know you are at the end of your rope. Your body language (not to mention your ashen and blotchy skin) speaks volumes without a single word spoken.

Children become afraid when they see anger. It is not good for children of any age to see you solve your challenges this way. If you have a tendency to swear, yell, throw things or other acts of violence, obviously your behavior has to change or you could be receiving guests at your local day spa called county jail. Begin with thinking clearly.

Pull the plug on acting out. Your bad behavior is very intimidating and scary to a child. It is important that you remove yourself immediately from that environment or the surroundings even if it is only for a few minutes. These few minutes of reprieve will give you time to pull yourself together, gather your thoughts or ideas, spike your inhibitory nerves in the frontal lobe part of your brain—the reasoning and judgment sector.

Learn to talk constructively once you have pulled yourself together and do not launch into a detailed discussion that would usually last until the sun sets and rises the next morning.

Don't nag—any time of the day!

Say what you want to say when you are dealing with children but be brief. Do not spout your usual 5000-plus words in a verbal dissertation. Edit it to kindergarten lingo, 10 words or less. Just as the punishment should fit the crime, the conversation should fit the age of your child. It is common for parents to lecture on the pros and cons of the act and go completely overboard in getting their point across. Honestly, your child shuts down before you completed your first sentence. This is the perfect time when less is better!

Leave no room for misinterpretation. When you are dealing with adults speak in declarative sentences. Do not ramble on by repeating yourself over and over. You lose credibility and are downplaying the other person's intelligence and their ability to learn. Remember, as with dealing with children, don't nag—any time of the day or night! It is up to the person in your line of fire to ask questions of clarity.

Watch your mouth for inappropriate language and condescension while minding your P's and Q's.

I encourage my clients to **take some level of ownership** of the act because it defuses any existing hostilities, irritations or uneasiness that could be in the atmosphere. Even if you have been exonerated, stop and ask yourself: Did I get my point across? Did I also air my views and opinions? I have just convinced this non-negotiable, antagonistic person, that my way is best. What a great feeling! By using a good choice of words and a small amount of acquiescence, you just got what you wanted.

Oh sure, it is not going to work all the time. Sometimes people dig their heels in deeper. They are so set on their decision that nothing you can say or do that will change their mind. Your cue to walk away is now. Know that you tried your best and offered your greatest effort. It is just not to be. Remember, you cannot always have a custom-made-in-an-off-the-rack world.

Relax your mind and your body. You need to work on calming down. Just like everything else, you must really want to make it happen and to be successful, knowing that you will fail the first or second even your third try. The great automobile creator Henry Ford once said, *"Failure is an opportunity to begin again more intelligently."*

But how can I get this rage out of me? **Re-focus your mind.**

Whatever helps you get your harmony back in sync. Maybe enroll in a dance studios, health club or think of John Travolta dancing in *Saturday Night Fever*. Play relaxing music. I admit I am partial to *American Songbook* melodies. Then seek a comfortable position to sit.

Taking deep breaths is an essential practice because it helps you focus on the presence and flow of your energy. Begin with slow deep breaths in the through the nose, filling our lungs. Push the air out through your mouth. Pay attention to your expanding lungs and soften on the exhalation. As you become absorbed in your breathing, you become more aware of the sensations surrounding the rising and falling of your chest.

Deepen your focus, noticing the flow of air moving through the sinus cavities. You will feel the breath traveling through your nostrils, and on into your lungs and throat. When you are ready, shift your concentration from controlling your breathing to a memory that makes you smile, a happy memory. I visualize my children Sarah's and Scott's faces and remember funny situations we got ourselves into and the inevitable hysterical laughter later.

Rest and pause in that memory. When you notice your mind wandering bring it back again and again. Interject other pleasant memories. Do whatever it takes to keep you smiling while the soft music plays on.

Begin to relax your facial muscles. Then roll your shoulders, letting them relax. Continue on with your arms, belly, and lower back. Relax some more. Continue to work your way down to the tips of your toes. The more you relax, the more you feel the release of the rigidity, tightness and worry.

You have probably noticed by now that your rational mind that serves to compare, judge and seek understanding is becoming clear having been washed of tension, stagnation and stress. Depending on how stressed I feel, this exercise can take as long at 45 minutes or as little as 15.

Other ways of relieving stress could be running a few miles—but only after checking with your physician. Start walking. Take a hike or ride a bicycle. Whatever form of relief you use it is important to allow yourself to download. This is not going to happen overnight. Relaxation techniques take practice and consistency. Step outside your comfort zone and notice that your attitude is more pleasing and you will not be as volatile or hostile. You will not feel as drained.

Sense who you are. Who are you, really? Look at yourself without criticism or judgment. Be present to the process of your life unfolding moment by moment.

Now drain the emotional bathtub and stop drowning yourself. You are the one in the driver's seat of your life. It is your job to put petrol (gas) in your tank. Go out there and find opportunity and prosper.

Do You Make The Parental Grade?

Okay, so you would like to think you are a great parent.

Everyone says they are. How do you know if you are making the grade? What sets you apart from everyone else? What makes you an A+ parent? Is it what you do? Is it what you say?

A good parent might be seen as someone who is there for their children, no matter what. A good parent might be described as someone who sacrifices their own wants, needs and desires for their children and does not complain or assign blame. A good parent might be someone who willingly administers loving caring support. Some might even give up their life for their children.

Universally these ideas are ideally how parents see themselves and their performance in the role of parent. It is not that difficult to see. You already have the potential for being a good parent. All it takes is perseverance and consistency. You experience your share of ups and downs as much as any other parent. Raising children is not easy.

Some parents who are lousy at raising children generally find an escape. They tack it to their own historical traumatic experiences in years past. They choose to hold themselves hostage to their own forgotten childhood deficiencies. This is their excuse for poor parenting today. This is much easier rather than challenging themselves to overcome their pitiful childhood. With certainty, they believed their children would never experience the same loveless dominating father and weak, timid, brow-beaten mother.

Truth is they are more inadequate as adults because they were never given the proper tools as a child. To those people I say, "Now is the time to stop with the pity party." Cut out the bull and excuses. *Your past does not come close to equaling your future.* We have all had trauma or an experience we would just as soon forget.

Somehow your inner will and internal strength will carry you through. You can be successful in overcoming past trauma. You are a walking, functioning adult. When you resurrect the past you are holding yourself hostage, creating a more strenuous and difficult road to recovery. For your children's sake, begin to make yourself the best parent you can be.

Past painful experiences will be easy to overcome if you deposit those memories in the trash can. Some will be more difficult than others. Nevertheless, we can unanimously agree that whatever the experience was, it is now a "was"— not a "now." Move forward and away from the past for your sake and sanity.

This is the key: keep the past in the past because it has no place in the future. You really can become a poster parent, a stronger person, by allowing all the past bad experiences to remain in the past. It's history. Give it up!

Whether or not you have children you can still be a better person. If it applies to being an outstanding parent, so much the better! Remember those moments of marvel when you saw the expression on someone's face because you treated them with dignity? You treated them with respect and never expect anything in return. You got the reward, the good grade. That grade is reflected in the glow of pleasure or the radiant happiness in a person's face because you were kind to them. Isn't that worth an A?

We are very selfish as a society and equally self-indulgent in our personal lives and we continue to allow it to happen. People consistently take the easy way out. You have all the comforts of technology, the ability to communicate or not even from a distance. You allow yourself to lose the feeling of goodness. Everybody wants something from each encounter. When the expectations fall short many become mean or hostile. That's an F in my grading system.

"I'm not going to allow you to come between my boyfriend and me!" I once heard a mother tell her daughter.

What an instant way to make a teenage girl feel unimportant and worthless! As a divorced mother of two teenagers, I, too, can only beg you to not get lost in the fog of selfishness. *It's all about me! What's in it for me? If I do this for you, what do I get in return?* These are but a few statements today's generation is grossly familiar with. Teens and adults respond more to a positive upbeat tone. We are more apt to accommodate, cooperate and collaborate with contentment. We will not be mired down with resentment when choosing to exhibit an act of being pleasant.

Adults, teenagers and young children believe that when they have your full attention they are being listened to and heard. Their opinion matters and has meaning. Their thoughts are being considered and validated.

You cannot treat a teenager like a child any more. They are not. But they are not adults yet either. Teenagers have developed their own opinions, thoughts and views. We may not always agree with their viewpoint. That is for sure. Nevertheless, we, as parents, must open our mind to the next generation that is evolving into independent individuals just like us, but they need our wisdom and direction.

Step-Parenting—But Still Making The Grade

Statistically speaking people who get married again and have children or plan to co-mingle families have a lesser chance of survival. Sixty-five percent of second marriages fail. Why? No one wants to grow old by themselves. They do not like being alone day after day. They need financial security or sadly use some other self-serving purpose.

I cannot stress the importance of giving yourself at least two years to get to know each other before introductions begin with your children. Then *only* if you believe your significant other has a greater than 99.99999% chance of being "a keeper," and, of course, "until death do you part" in your equation. Introductions which come too soon open the door for premature attachment and bonding. Should your relationship go sour, remember your first marriage and how your children felt and suffered when it ended.

If you choose to ignore all the signs the most common explanation for failed marriages after the first one is the step-parent is allowed to take on the role of disciplinarian with the biological parent standing by, allowing it to happen. Much to the children's detriment, they now, with a heart full of resentment must learn a new set of rules and regulations set down by their new step-parent.

On the upside you have taken the time and gradually and cautiously introduced to your "keeper," coupled with lots of listening and positive communication, then what? You want to get married! I strongly suggest that you do not rush it.

Take time to consider the children's feelings, allowing them to be involved with the co-mingling of families and any arrangements and plans to be made. Permit all the children to air their thoughts and ideas. Give each child a task. Their involvement will dissolve or lessen any resentment, stress or hiccup you might face later. The objective is to never allow the children to feel disconnected from you in any way or outcast because you made the decision to move into a new life and title.

"I hate my stepfather," a 15-year-old girl declared to me in a session. Strong, hateful words coming from someone so young, I thought. Over the course of a month and several hours of conversation later, I discovered why this young lady had such vengeful thoughts of her stepfather.

I met Jan's stepfather, Tom. He was a tall, muscular man who genuinely had a concern as to why Jan disliked him. He could not understand why someone as kind and generous as he was, could even remotely be disliked by anyone. As the sessions progressed, it was revealed that Jan s mother was Tom's third wife! Tom had children from his first and second marriages. How many and with whom was unclear. Tom was evasive and would quickly change the subject when asked questions on his historical events.

There was a great deal of family co-mingling going on. Jan's mother apparently did not know there were several other children floating around who were all fathered by Tom. Jan's mother and Tom dated for six and a half months before they got married. To compound the challenge, Jan's younger brother Steven only met Tom three or four times during the courtship. Only two of Tom's children were present at the wedding. Tom did not offer an explanation as to where his other children were.

It is not hard to see why Jan was struggling. Jan was overly protecting, her mother, becoming almost mother-like herself. Jan's mother jumped into this marriage because of her own fear of growing old alone. Jan feels that if her mother had taken more time to get to know Tom she would have discovered that Tom not only has two children but four others!

To add insult to injury, neither Jan nor her brother Steven were asked by their mother their opinion of Tom. Did they like him? Would he be a good fit for the family? Does he seem honest and honorable? Does he have a good character and integrity? They were never allowed to express their thoughts. The invalidation and lack of control in this situation was obvious for Jan and her brother Steven. Their mother was desperate.

Besides dealing with her mother's poor judgments and choices in men, Jan and Steven, are living primarily with their mother. They must also live with Tom every hour of every day as their new step-parent. They must live with a man who is deceitful and vague.

Because the "warm fuzzies" did not exist between Tom and Jan prior to the marriage, Jan and Steven have built up resistance and resentment to their stepfather. What else could anyone expect? Naturally any attempt by Tom to enforce discipline is ignored or at the very least, challenged.

"He's not my father. I have a real dad. Only my Mom and Dad have the right to discipline me." These are the most common and frequently heard words uttered from co-mingled families. You could be the best step-parent, but the fact of the matter is the child's loyalties are going to be with his or her biological parents first. Step-parents who force their way into a child's life are absolutely going to hit a brick wall of resistance.

When you become a step-parent you are trying so hard to be accepted. But nothing seems to be working. Stop!

Relationships are not supposed to be this difficult. Take a breath and a step back. Recognize that this child has parents to whom he or she is loyal. You do not want to set yourself up for failure by mercilessly enforcing your viewpoints and unfamiliar tactics. The last thing you want to do is help to reinforce the wall of resentment and bitterness with steel. What you do want is for that wall to dissolve like sugar.

If you choose to combine families your primary focus is on your own children and not the stepchildren. Be there for them all when they need your emotional support or need some comfort. But when it comes to the raising or your stepchildren with discipline, medical issues and finances, steer clear and stay quiet. Leave these issues up to the biological parents unless it directly impacts you. Stay behind the scenes.

I have had many families come into my office, eliciting deep discussions about how the children are not cooperative and disrespectful to their step-parent. When push comes to shove what is really needed to be done was for the step-parent to back off a little. Remember, you are a *spouse*. That is where your role ends. It would be outrageous of you to assume any other role than step-parent unless there is no biological mother or father in the child's life.

Single Parents

A single parent is defined as a parent who has never been married. If you were once married and you are now divorced, you are a *divorced* parent. Do not sugar-coat it.

Whether you are a single or divorced parent it is the most difficult type of parenting because you are doing everything alone. Oh, you may have the support of your family if they live close to you. If you do not have family support then you are a lone soldier doing your best to raise outstanding decent moral children. Quite an assignment for any parent!

To raise children of morality and character you must be an outstanding moral family valued parent yourself. How well I know! I speak from experience. I want to share with you my experience of being a divorced parent of two well-adjusted teenagers. Perhaps you will indulge me and learn something from my story.

My former husband and I split up in May 1991. My children were four and five years old. I was a stay-at-home mum until my marriage crumbled. I thought if got a job it would help us, financially and maybe, just maybe my marriage could be saved.

I found employment pretty quick, but that meant my children had to be in a daycare facility. My heart cried a thousand tears each time I left them behind in this institution I resented, watching those little faces on the other side of the glass begging me not to leave them behind. It tore me apart. I hated it. I felt so alone, lost and empty, my whole world was being completely turned upside down.

I was in a perpetual mental and emotional tizzy. The last place I should have been was at a fulltime job. But I had to work or so I thought in order to make financial ends meet. Two months or so into this job I realized that I was losing sight of what was important to me: my wonderful children.

I walked into my boss's office that Thursday afternoon and informed him that I could not longer perform the duties he required of me because my duties were to be home raising my children and I left. Just like that. Job (and stress) gone. It all ended.

When my children started kindergarten, I took a part-time job where I worked three hours a day when my children were in school. Once again the familiar air of not having much money was upon me. On many occasions my children ate dinner and I did not.

I remembered back to my childhood when my parents struggled with money and the three of us, Tommy, Elizabeth and I would eat but my parents did not, because there was not enough food to go around. Thirty years later, here I am doing the same thing with my children, making sure they have a roof over their heads a clean and warm bed to sleep in, clothes on the back and food in their belly. This is my job!

I brought them into the world and until the day I leave this earth I will damned well take care of them no matter how much I had to sacrifice!

Our children are like pets. You love them and feed them and they will *always* come back for more. Never under estimate the undying love and loyalty you receive when you give it unconditionally. You took care of them when they were just babies. You raised them to become well-rounded adults.

Since you have been a role model, mentor, confidant, and all around good parent, it will all come back to you. When you are old and gray, sitting in your rocking chair by the fireplace, reminiscing about your years past, unable to do the many thing you used to do, those wonderful children of yours will be first in line to care for you as when you took care of them. What goes around comes around. Isn't that the truth?

So is it an A or an F on *Your* Parent Report Card?

You have the potential to be a good divorced parent, step-parent or single parent. You must find the right mix by open communication, setting boundaries, offering consistency, giving and earning respect. You have the right to call yourself a good parent or you can do something about your failure. Are you an "A" parent? Or is there a note saying, "room for improvement?"

Take a look in the mirror and if you're brave enough to open yourself up to vulnerability. Ask your children, "Are there any areas where I could improve?" "Is there something I do that's upsetting to you?" "What is it I do that you like or dislike?"

You get the idea? However your child responds do not defend yourself! If it is something you do not like, learn from it. How your child sees you is the only grade that counts. Children speak from their hearts and if they can open themselves up to controversy by sharing their feelings and thoughts the least you can do is listen objectively. Take it and improve on it and if it is reasonable, of course. If everything said about you is good, then you get an *"A."*

What's So Great
About You?

I am a Scot. From the old country, you know. I was born in a small industrial town called Paisley; approximately 30 miles outside of Glasgow, but my formative years were in East Kilbride, 17 miles to the East. My dad has always been a hard worker for his family. In retirement he still works tirelessly, fixing and repairing things in my home each and every time my parents come to visit.

My Mum was blessed to be the matriarch of the house—and in the lush garden out back, too, for that matter. Mum worked up until one week before my brother Tommy was born in 1958. I came along two years later and then wee sister Elizabeth completed the family five years after me.

Our childhood was very fulfilling, full of laughter, and road trips in our green Ford Prefect, which on a good day the top speed of this hot rod was 35 mph. We nicknamed it *The Green Flash*.

My family did not have a lot of money when we were growing up. There were many times my parents went without evening dinner because there was not enough food to go around all five of us. But we always had clothes on our backs, food in our bellies and loving parents who provided for us in the best way they knew how.

My parents disciplined us in a way that most parents shy from today. When we stepped out of line we got slapped on the bare bum, the thigh, or the back of our hands. Never did the thought of Child Protective Services being summoned enter my parents minds. The worse punishment of all was *"you wait until your Dad gets home…"* Mum's words put the fear of impending death in me.

As a child you imagine your life is going to end that night, *when your Dad gets home,* echoing torture and horror in my mind. I would sit and sweat nervously, furrowing a trail in the carpet from the sofa to the window, watching for *The Green Flash* of doom, pull up into the driveway. But more often than not, those words I feared were simply just words. When Dad did get home the punishment had already been administered. You see, it was the anticipation of impending torture, mayhem and eventual execution, the fear that I would not live to see tomorrow.

Even though we were growing up peacefully in a nation across The Pond, our home was probably similar to most American homes. We experienced our share of humps and bumps as we all grew older with family supporting each other, conquering those obstacles of sibling arguments, coupled with not being allowed to say out all night.

Our daily lives which appeared squashed by parental influences were actually blessings that have shaped each one of us to surpass any imaginable expectation of greatness. Whether your greatness is self-inflicted or implanted by parental influences, as in our case, it is there and has always been. Tommy and Elizabeth agree.

Everyone has something they can do far better than anyone else. But where do you *find* greatness? You don't. No one will walk down the street and find greatness lying on the pavement in a big heap. Greatness is nurtured from within. "But how do I nurture my greatness if I don't know what it is or where to look?" you ask.

Separate greatness into the categories of physical, emotional, verbal and mental.

I asked this question of many men and women, of all ages, ethnic backgrounds, shapes, sizes and religions. "In your opinion, what makes a person *great?*"

Not surprisingly, most women responded with an emotionally-based opinion because that is what most women do, react and make decisions on their emotions, not what is factual or visual. Men's opinions are verbal and physically visual.

The Woman's Response

"A great person should be kind and thoughtful; a person who listens and hears every word you said; a great person is someone who's there for you emotionally."
Erika

"A great person is someone who is not afraid to tell you that you're wrong; a person who listens and shares ideas and thoughts; someone who doesn't say mean hurtful things about you."
Julie

"A great person is someone who is happy most of the time; a person who will tell you the truth, even when the truth may hurt; someone who tries to make you feel better if you're sad, and has compassion for others."
Sarah

"Someone who is respectful and honest, a person of good character and values; a great person is someone who can step out-side of themselves and not have a self-serving hidden agenda."
Marcia

These responses are predominantly *emotionally-based* with little reference to inner strength and physical appearance. Notwithstanding, they carry a tremendous amount of value and worth to the person seeking *greatness*.

The Man's Response

"A great person is someone who will not back down in a negotiation; a person who follows through on what they said, or walks the walk and talks the talk; a person who

stands tall in belief."
Kevin

"Someone with integrity and value for others; a person who cares about other people and has compassion and self-worth; a person who can stand up for their rights and those of others…"
Ed

"Someone with their own personality; they're not trying to be someone else; they have their own unique characteristics; someone who is honest and mature, someone who takes the time to learn about others."
Scott

It is not a surprise that men are more physical and visual than women. No need to be discouraged, ladies. You can be physical and visual like the men. And for the record, men, it would not hurt to be in touch with your "feminine side" once in a while.

Everyone wants to be each one of these definitions. You can do it. Honestly, you can. Girl Guide's Honor! If you go for one then why not for the whole jackpot? But know that it takes time and the willingness to take a step back and a look in the mirror. You need to acknowledge that the perfect person does not exist, *anywhere*. Everyone has flaws, pieces of them they want to improve, myself included. There is greatness to be found in building, so let's get the construction tools out and build.

First you must recognize the areas for improvement. Is it *your* attitude? Is it your negative choices of words? Do you have a short fuse? Whatever it is it needs identifying. Open yourself up to construction by asking your family and close friends to help you identify the areas that need modification.

If your family and friends are courageous enough to share their opinions, knowing there is a huge chance that you will become huffy with them, the least you can do is courageously want to fix it and without bitterness. Start with purposely catching yourself before you carry out an act that could be viewed as destructive. Pay attention to your actions. Remember that actions always speak louder than words. Stop yourself before you become physically, emotionally, verbally and mentally abusive.

View yourself as a warrior and a creator. You are your own toolbox. Be willing to set aside your ego and open your eyes to your new adventure on becoming a great person. If you choose to stay blind, how will you ever be able to see the road ahead?

Greatness is like happiness. *It is a way of life, not a destination.* Everyone has the potential to be more than they believed they could ever be. It is there inside you. You already have it so why not let it grow? Treat it like a plant that needs nurturing. The food and water are kind words, compassion and selflessness. A gift from you!

To illustrate the point, I will share these letters from two damaged people, afraid to look in the mirror because of what they might see. The upside is they found the strength to turn themselves around. If they can do it, so can you.

Dear Ms. Neeley,

What you said to me really got me thinking about relationships and my admission to taking more than I was giving. Thank you for reminding me that there really is life after divorce. Most women after divorce seem to think there is nothing left for them to offer the world. You are the exception and I admire your courage to grow and learn. I admire your confidence and your will to go get what you want without hurting others in your path.

Dear Caroline:

Thank you for taking the time to share with me that I should never be afraid to try something new or challenge myself to do better. You asked me, "How will you know how good you are if you don't give it a try?" Each day I challenge myself more, my attitude is better and I communicate with enthusiasm, I have more friends than I thought I would ever have.

These people believed they were damaged beyond repair. Clearly I disagreed. They were also at a point in their life where they were losing control of themselves. They realized that if they did not seek some intervention they were heading down the path of complete and absolute destruction. Every day that went by without action the closer destruction became. What these people needed was to find someone who was willing to listen to their tale and not be afraid to point out their flaws regardless of the consequences.

Whether you are the tale teller or tale receiver, what is important is the motivation and drive to either change yourself or help someone with the process. As chilling as it might be to look in the mirror you must do it—even though you may see a scary monster. But remember, you can be the slayer of the monster. The only way you can become that person is by facing your fear head on just as the two letter writers did. That *is* what makes you great!

WHEREVER I GO, SOMEONE ASKS A QUESTION

Having been in this business and on the radio for some time now wherever I go, undoubtedly someone will approach me with a question.

"Excuse me, are you Caroline Neeley? I wonder if I might have one minute of your time to ask you a personal question." This is generally how it goes. And naturally I offer a possible solution to their issue or concern.

Of course, I do not mind using up some of my "off" time when I am alone but if I am with my family or friends, I really only can give them a few minutes. I truly care but I do not want to take away time from whomever I am with at the time. Seems fair enough, right? When I am on the air it is important to stay focused on getting the *real* question asked. I can then respond using minimum time, choosing a helpful answer and allowing me to get to as many calls as possible.

The questions vary drastically. Some revolve around a family issue or a protective move regarding their divorce or a heartbreaking question about how to move forward from a death. Most common though, people often ask me a personal question. If it is not too invasive I am more than willing to assist.

Here are some random, interesting questions and my no-holds-barred response. I have also thrown in some not so favorable statements for your entertainment, and how I responded so you can learn should you find yourself in similar situations. I received these letters by either email or fax.

Q.   My father didn't walk me down the aisle. Our wedding started at 11:00

a.m. My son walked me to the altar instead. My father arrived when we were halfway through the vows. He was very upset and angry that we did not wait for him. He created a scene by shouting "Who's in charge here?" My father hasn't spoken to me since the wedding. Do you have any suggestions?

A.   *Do you want your father to be in your children's life when you have them?* ("Yes," she replied.) *You can't force your father to speak to you. If you want to establish a relationship with him again, I suggest this. Phone him and ask him to have coffee or tea with you, just the two of you. When you see him, give him a tight cuddle and tell him how much you've missed him. Then explain how important and exciting your wedding day was. Express your sorrow for not waiting longer for him on your wedding day. Give your father the opportunity to explain his side of the story, what the delay was, and hope that he will take ownership for his behavior, too. If he refuses to back down, even a wee bit, consider it his loss, because clearly he doesn't understand what he will miss in your life.*

Obviously, this young lady feels badly for the chain reaction of events that occurred on the most important day of her life. She is also feeling the loss of her father's physical and emotional presence.

What I am suggesting to her is 1) acknowledge that both father and daughter were a bit too hasty with their actions; 2) move beyond the emotional hurt; 3) imagine the rest of her life without the soothing sound of her father's voice and the endless stream of his love and support. Her final endeavor is to take ownership and responsibility for her lack of patience and offer her father the opportunity to do the same.

Q.   My husband and I have been married for 11 years and we have no children. Since our marriage vows he has had two affairs. After catching him for the second time he swore to me he wouldn't do it again. I forgave him the first time but the second time? Of course, I have doubts. Can you give me a sense of direction? I am hopelessly lost!

A.   *Thank goodness there are no children to mimic his disrespectful behavior. Your husband lost his trust and loyalty with you on his first affair but to turn around and do it again? In my opinion, once a cheater, always a cheater. If I were you, I would put a clean pair of knickers and his toothbrush in a brown paper bag, put it on the front door step and tell him that "I'll see you in court." And remember even if you were the worst person to live with in the whole western hemisphere, no one deserves that kind of disrespect.*

Q.   I am in my late 40s and have been remarried for a year and a half. My former wife lives in the same town. My 16-year-old daughter does not like my current wife and is upset with me for marrying her so soon after divorcing her mother. How can I get my daughter to come visit us more and also stop being upset with me?

A.   *You can't make her come see you more. These things take time. You cared less about her feelings and how she interacted with your then-fiancé and more about getting married again. You have got some explaining to do as to why you moved on so quickly and disregarded her. She feels left behind and abandoned by you. I suggest you begin with asking her to have lunch or dinner, just the two of you. Take her to the movies or indulge her with your presence and less on your own wants, needs and desires. When she asks you questions about the divorce from her mother, and your new marriage, be completely honest and open with your answer. She is old enough to understand and deserves the truth. If you want her in your life you're going to have to chase her and make her "want" to be with you. And when the time is right, slowly re-introduce your new wife.*

Q.

I have a 17-year-old son who I suspect is smoking marijuana. He says
he is not smoking anymore. Do I
have the right to search his room?

A.

*Yes, if you suspect he's up to no good
and could harm himself. Absolutely!
You have the right. If he were to get
busted or cause harm to someone
through being stoned and the police
found out you knew about his addiction and did nothing, you could be
prosecuted. You and your son could
have a picnic in county jail!*

Q.

I heard you say on one radio show
that some people call you a
"b-i-t-c-h".

Why do they think that?

A.

*Because I'm self-assured, and confident.
I speak my mind and I hold people
accountable for their actions. It's much
easier for people to blame someone else,
and when you have someone like me
calling you on it, people don't like it. I
might add that I thank people for the*

*compliment. Puzzled, they tell me it was not meant as one. I continue the conversation with "B.I.T.C.H." is an acronym for **B**abe **I**n **T**otal **C**ontrol of **H**erself. Thank you very much.*

Q.   When your children were younger, how did you manage on your own and as a divorced mother of two?

A.   *Children never ask for a divorce. I believe it is just as hard on the children as it is on their parents. Nevertheless, I had a choice to make. Was I going to sink or swim? Obviously, I chose to swim. With that, it became my job even more to help myself and my children through this difficult time in our lives. I worked when they were in school and was home when they got home. I attended all their school and sporting events and performances. But most importantly, I showered them with love and affection and told them thousands of times how important they are to me.*

Yes, at times my single life was incredibly overwhelming and often I felt lost. It is not easy being a divorced mother. When I look at how my two babies have turned out—respectful, loyal, good personalities and impeccable characters—all the tears, loneliness and fear of the unknown was worth it. All the love and support I have given comes right back, but twice as much and with twice the power. For that, I am very grateful.

MY HOPE FOR YOU

Congratulations! Good for you! You made it all the way to end of this book. I hope you enjoyed the reading and by now have uncovered your hidden attributes and fired the detriments—never to be seen again.

My goal for you is simple. You have experienced many trials and tribulations in your life. Probably no more than anyone else has but what makes you a stronger more self-assured and self-assertive individual is that you are now more willing and able to fight for what is rightfully yours and do "what's in the best interest of…"

Always remember you only have the power to change the things you have control over. What you see is what you are going to get. Then ask yourself, "Can I live with that even though it does not meet my standards?" Or would you rather continue to build on your newly discovered ***Glasgow Kiss*** attitude? Life is black and white. The gray area is only a place someone goes to when they do not want to deal with the black and white of life.

Your life is full of choices and you are the one in the driver's seat. The only direction you need and where you want to go will come from you. If something does not feel right, smell right, look right, then chances are it is not right. So do not do it.

> Try extra hard not to complicate your issues or dissect them too much by looking for something that didn't exist in the first place.

> We can all learn from our mistakes.

> Do not lose sight of the simpler things in life.

I want you to remember once in awhile that:

> You will learn humility by being humiliated.

> You will learn honesty by being honest.

And I really hope that you will *not* get a brand new car when you are 16.

It is life-changing when at least once you can see puppies born and your old dog put to sleep.

I hope you get a black eye fighting for something you believe in.

When you want to see a movie and your little brother or sister wants to tag along, I hope you'll let him or her join you just this once. You are their hero.

Allow your children to dig in the dirt and make a fort out of bed sheets.

When you learn to use computers I hope you also learn to add and subtract in your head.

When you swear or talk back to your Mum I hope you learn what Ivory© soap tastes like.

May you skin your knee climbing a mountain, burn your hand on a stove and stick your tongue on a frozen flagpole! Celebrate!

When a friend offers you dope or a joint I hope you realize he is *not* your friend.

Make time to sit and talk with your Granny and Grandpa. They were young once themselves.

These things I wish for you: Stay in touch with reality. Keep your feet on the ground. To me it is the only way to appreciate life.

Always tell your family and the friends you value to cherish this: "We secure our relationships, not by accepting favors but by doing them. I am always here for you and if I die first I'll go to heaven and wait for you."

It is all up to you. Now get going. Life is out there, waiting on you!

From The Heart

Dear Mum,

Thanks for all your hugs and kisses
Thanks for all the times you wiped our tears,
Thanks for the open ears and open heart
Thanks for the shoulder to lean on
Thanks for being you, the best Mum ever!

—Sarah and Scott, your babies

About the Author

Caroline Neeley was born and raised in Scotland, setting foot on American soil on January 9, 1980.

A divorced mother of two, Caroline's dream of being self-employed was realized when she hit the business world as an independent Mediator and Anger Management Counselor in southern California in October 2000. Her mission is to consistently take a non-partisan, unbiased approach to all disputes and unresolved matters with her *"Glasgow Kiss"* attitude and no-holds-barred realistic techniques.

Caroline has strong ideas and convictions, never hesitating to voice them when men and women do irresponsible things to disrupt or damage themselves and others happiness.

Her dry Scottish humor and compassion for others makes people want to kick off their shoes and relax in the comfort of her cozy office.

She is an award-winning entrepreneur, radio talk show host, avid runner and lives in southern California with her daughter Sarah, son Scott and four well-adjusted cats.

978-0-595-38577-5
0-595-38577-X

Printed in the United States
46439LVS00001BA/1-219